W9-BLD-614

The Science of Living Things

What are WETLANDS?

Bobbie Kalman & Amanda Bishop

Crabtree Publishing Company

www.crabtreebooks.com

The Science of Living Things Series
A Bobbie Kalman Book

Dedicated by Amanda Bishop
For the folks at the NFPL Boys & Girls Department

Editor-in-Chief
Bobbie Kalman

Editorial director
Niki Walker

Writing team
Bobbie Kalman
Amanda Bishop

Research
Molly Aloian

Editor
Kathryn Smithyman

Copy editor
Rebecca Sjonger

Art director
Robert MacGregor

Design
Kymberly McKee Murphy
Katherine Kantor

Production coordinator
Heather Fitzpatrick

Photo researcher
Laura Hysert

Consultant
Patricia Loesche, Ph.D., Animal Behavior Program,
Department of Psychology, University of Washington

Photographs and reproductions
Frank S. Balthis: pages 22 (top), 30 (bottom), 31
Erwin and Peggy Bauer: pages 17, 18-19
James Kamstra: page 8
Robert McCaw: pages 5 (bottom), 15 (bottom), 16 (bottom)
McDonald Wildlife Photography, Inc.: Joe McDonald: page 30 (top)
Allen Blake Sheldon: pages 6, 15 (top), 16 (top), 20, 27 (top)
Tom Stack & Associates: Brian Parker: page 23
Michael Turco: pages 9 (top), 24
Visuals Unlimited: Charlie Heidecker: page 28;
    Glenn M. Oliver: page 10 (bottom);
    Rick Poley: page 25;
    Fritz Pölking: page 21 (top)
Other images by Adobe Image Library, Corbis Images, Digital Stock
and Digital Vision

Illustrations
Barbara Bedell: pages 8 (top), 16, 22, 28 (top)
Katherine Kantor: pages 7, 10 (top), 12 (right), 13, 14, 18 (top), 20,
    24 (bottom), 25, 26, 30, 31
Margaret Amy Reiach: pages 4 (top), 12 (left), 18 (bottom), 24 (top)
Bonna Rouse: pages 4 (bottom), 6, 8 (bottom), 10 (bottom), 12 (top), 28 (middle)

Crabtree Publishing Company

www.crabtreebooks.com   1-800-387-7650

Cataloging-in-Publication Data
Kalman, Bobbie.
  What are wetlands?/Bobbie Kalman & Amanda Bishop.
    p. cm. -- (The science of living things series)
Includes index.
This book investigates some types of wetlands, including swamps, marshes,
bogs, and fens; the many plants and animals that live in wetlands; and the
threats to these ecosystems.
  ISBN 0-86505-993-4 (RLB) -- ISBN 0-86505-970-5 (pbk.)
  1. Wetland ecology--Juvenile literature. 2. Wetlands--Juvenile literature. [1.
Wetlands. 2. Wetland ecology. 3. Ecology.] I. Bishop, Amanda. II. Title. III.
Science of living things.
  QH541.5.M3 B57 2003
  577.68--dc21
                                                          LC 2002012125

**Published in
the United States**

PMB16A
350 Fifth Ave.
Suite 3308
New York, NY
10118

**Published
in Canada**

616 Welland Ave.
St. Catharines, Ontario
L2M 5V6

**Published in the
United Kingdom**

White Cross Mills
High Town, Lancaster
LA1 4XS

**Published
in Australia**

386 Mt. Alexander Rd.
Ascot Vale (Melbourne)
VIC 3032

Contents

What are wetlands?

Wetlands are areas of land that are wet for at least part of the year. Some are covered with up to six feet (2 m) of water year-round. Others are underwater only at certain times of the year. In some wetlands, water does not sit on the ground, but the soil is **waterlogged**, or full of water.

Wetlands form when water collects on land. The water may be fresh or **saline**. Saline water is salty. The four main types of freshwater wetlands are marshes, swamps, fens, and bogs. Saline wetlands include salt marshes and mangrove swamps. Each of these wetlands is home to a variety of plants and animals.

Water sources

The water in wetlands may come from one source or from many different sources. **Groundwater** bubbles up through the soil from underground, creating springs and pools. **Precipitation** is water that falls from the sky as rain or snow. When a lot of precipitation falls and is not absorbed by the ground, it helps create **runoff**, or water that moves along the earth's surface from one area to another. Runoff also includes water flowing from groundwater sources.

*Runoff from heavy rainfall can feed a wetland or even form a new one if a **depression**, or dip, in the soil collects water.*

Waterlogged land

Water can slip through even the tiniest holes and cracks in soil. The land in wetlands, however, traps water and causes it to **accumulate**, or collect. An underground layer of solid rock, called **bedrock**, stops the water from seeping through the ground and draining away. Instead, the water builds up and fills all the tiny spaces in the soil, making it waterlogged. Sometimes the water also forms **aquifers**, or underground pools, on the bedrock.

Water on land

Wetlands are found in every part of the world except Antarctica. Many wetlands form where lakes, rivers, and oceans meet land. Wetlands can develop almost anywhere, however, as long as there is enough water to keep the soil waterlogged.

Fresh water

All living things need fresh water to survive—even those that live in saline wetlands! Both groundwater and precipitation are freshwater sources. The **water cycle**, shown right, moves fresh water through the environment.

Getting wet

The water cycle helps ensure that all wetlands have a supply of fresh water for the plants and animals that live in them. Many wetlands stay waterlogged year-round, but **seasonal** wetlands dry up for part of the year, when there is not enough precipitation to keep their soils soaked. The water cycle keeps groundwater and precipitation in constant movement, so that even seasonal and **inland** wetlands, or wetlands that do not form on shores, have a steady supply of fresh water.

Nature's filters

Water that enters wetlands is often **polluted**. As it moves along the earth, runoff picks up chemicals such as **pesticides**. Air pollution creates **acid rain**, which harms plants and animals. Some wetland plants, such as pickerelweed (right), help clean the water in a wetland. They filter water as it enters wetlands and draw out chemicals. Many plants also absorb acid, keeping the water safe for other wetland inhabitants.

How water moves

As water travels through the environment, its temperature changes many times. At different temperatures, water changes form. In cold temperatures, liquid water freezes into solid ice. When heated, ice melts into liquid. Heated liquid water **evaporates** into a gas called **vapor**. Vapor **condenses** to liquid when it is cooled.

The water cycle is closely related to the **climate**, or the long-term weather conditions, of an area. For example, in a cool area where a lot of rain falls, water evaporates very slowly, so there is often a lot of liquid water at the ground level. A bog may form in these conditions (see pages 20-21). Different wetlands form in other climates, depending on how the climate affects the water cycle in those areas.

Water vapor condenses and forms clouds when it gets cold. When enough vapor collects, it falls to the Earth as precipitation.

When precipitation lands, some soaks into the ground, some runs off into bodies of water, and some is absorbed by plant roots.

*Plants **transpire**, or release, extra water back into the sky as vapor. Water also evaporates from the surface of water bodies. All vapor travels upward, where it forms clouds and falls as precipitation, starting the water cycle over again.*

Wetland plants

Common reeds are emergents. They can grow to heights of ten feet (3 m) above the water.

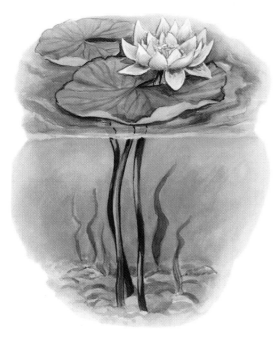

Floating plants, such as this water lily, have leaves that float on the surface and take in air. The air moves down the hollow stem to the roots.

The waterlogged soil found in wetlands is called **hydric** soil. Only certain types of plants, called **hydrophytes**, can grow in this soggy soil. The word "hydrophyte" comes from the Greek words for "water" and "lover." Some hydrophytes, such as pondweed, are **submerged**, or live totally underwater. Floating hydrophytes, such as water hyacinths, sit on the water's surface. **Emergents**, such as cattails, are rooted in underwater soil, but most of their parts grow above water.

Getting enough air

All plants need air to help their different parts function. Air contains gases such as **carbon dioxide**, which plants need in order to survive. Hydric soil is so full of water, however, that it does not have much space for air. Hydrophytes have special features that help them get enough air to survive. Some have air pockets in their leaves that allow them to float on the water's surface and take in air. Many plants have hollow tubes that connect their parts above the water to their parts below it. Air travels down these tubes.

Gathering soil

Plants play an important role during the early stages of wetland formation. The first plants to take root on the floor of a body of water are emergents such as rushes and reeds. They reproduce quickly, and many soon grow. The emergents **resist** the flow of water, causing it to swirl and slow down. Fast-moving water carries **sediment**, or small bits of soil, rock, and plants. When the water slows down, the sediment sinks to the bottom. It settles and collects around the roots of the emergents.

Shallow water

Water becomes shallower as sediment builds up on the bottom of the water body. The process by which sediment accumulates to make water shallower is called **terrestrialization**. If enough sediment builds up, plants that can survive only in shallow water are able to live in the new soil among the emergents. Before long, several types of hydrophytes start to grow in the area, and a wetland is formed.

*Few trees can survive a wetland's soggy conditions. Swamp trees such as cypresses are well suited to life in the water. Heavy **knees**, or bases, steady the trees against the water's flow.*

This frog is surrounded by duckweed, which is the world's smallest flowering plant.

9

Animal life

The yellow-billed stork is a wetland bird. Its long legs and bill help it wade in shallow water so it can catch fish.

Wetlands are home to a wide variety of animals that often are not found anywhere else. The animals range in size from **microscopic** creatures to large **reptiles** such as alligators and **mammals** such as manatees. Wetland animals include thousands of types of spiders, worms, insects, and small **crustaceans** such as crabs, shrimps, and crayfish. Fish enter wetlands through the streams or lakes that feed the areas. Birds, rodents, snakes, turtles, salamanders, and frogs find food and shelter among the plants and pools of wetlands.

They're everywhere!

No matter where a wetland is located, there is one insect—the mosquito—that will likely make its home there. Mosquitoes live in almost all wetlands, whether they are fresh or saline, hot or cold. Mosquitoes can even survive in the traps of meat-eating pitcher plants (see page 21)! Insects usually get digested in the leaves of pitcher plants, but mosquitoes are able to **breed** in them!

Living in and around water

Wetland animals must be suited to living in wet conditions. Like all animals, they need to breathe **oxygen** and must find enough food to survive. Fish have breathing organs called gills that allow them to breathe oxygen underwater. Some aquatic insects and spiders can form bubbles of air around their bodies, which they then use to breathe while moving underwater! Wetland birds and mammals hold their breath underwater and then breathe when they break the water's surface. **Amphibians** are completely at home in wetlands because these animals spend part of their lives in water and the other part on land.

Frogs are amphibians that live in or near wetlands. The wet surroundings help keep their skin from drying out.

Just visiting

Many animals do not live in wetlands full time, but they visit them to find water and food. All kinds of animal species, including a large number of birds, breed and raise their young in wetlands. Many birds also stop for a rest as they **migrate**, or travel, between their winter and summer homes. They often hide their nests among emergents and give birth there.

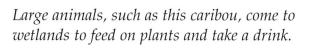

Large animals, such as this caribou, come to wetlands to feed on plants and take a drink.

Wetland communities

Photosynthesis

Leaves release oxygen and water vapor.

The sun shines on leaves.

Leaves absorb carbon dioxide from the air.

*Roots absorb water and **nutrients** from the soil.*

*Every **food chain** starts with the sun, which provides plants with the energy they need to make food.*

Wetlands are **ecosystems**. An ecosystem is made up of the plants, animals, and climate in an area. Every living thing in a wetland depends on the plants and animals around it for survival. For example, wetland plants provide food and shelter for many animals. Some animals help wetland plants by **pollinating** them or by spreading their seeds so new plants can grow. When the plants and animals live in balance, they keep the ecosystem healthy. If one part of the wetland community is removed, the rest of the ecosystem suffers.

Making food

Plants make their own food in a process called **photosynthesis**. They use energy from the sun to combine water with carbon dioxide. The process forms a type of sugar, which plants use for food. Photosynthesis also produces oxygen, which the plants release.

Links in the chain

The energy in wetland plants is passed on to all the animals in a wetland. Some animals get the energy directly by eating the plants. These animals are called **herbivores**. Other animals get some of the energy by eating the plant-eaters. These animals are **carnivores**, or meat-eaters. The links between wetland plants, herbivores, and carnivores make up food chains. Food chains also include tiny animals called **decomposers**. They feed on dead, decaying plants and animals. As they feed, they break down the plants and animals and help return their nutrients to the soil. These nutrients help new plants grow.

Marshes

Freshwater marshes are common wetlands. They form along the edges of lakes, rivers, and ponds. They may also form in shallow lakes, as emergent plants begin to grow along the edges and their roots collect sediment on the lake floor. Marshes are covered by water year-round.

Marshes, marshes, marshes!

Trees do not grow in marshes, but many other types of plants do. Emergents, including reeds, cattails, and bulrushes, grow close to shore. In deeper water, floating plants such as water lilies grow. As sediment builds up, other flowering plants begin to take root.

Marsh life

Marsh ecosystems support a wide variety of wildlife. Fish can live in marshes because the water stays all year. Underwater plant stems provide a safe place for fish, amphibians, and insects to lay eggs. The plants help hide the eggs from **predators**. Above the water, the tall, grassy plants also offer protection for birds, mammals, and reptiles that are nesting, raising young, or hiding from predators.

Muskrats are common marsh inhabitants.

*Bitterns are well **camouflaged** among marsh plants. When threatened, they stretch their necks and point their beaks upward. In this position, their brown-and-white bodies blend in with the reeds.*

Swamps

A swamp is a wetland where trees grow. It usually develops as soil builds up in a marsh and the water becomes shallow. In the shallowest parts of a swamp, the ground may dry up during warm seasons. The deepest parts of a swamp are covered by water year-round. Only some trees, such as ash, oak, maple, elm, and cypress, can survive in the deepest areas of a swamp, where their roots are covered by water. Swamps are usually named after the type of tress that grow in them.

Bring in the trees

Tree seeds cannot begin to grow when the soil is covered with water. In swamps, the water level drops when there is little rainfall. Some seeds fall on soil that is above the water level during these drier periods. They then take root in the soil among emergent plants and existing tree roots and begin to grow. Once the young trees are rooted, they can survive underwater for short periods of time, such as when runoff or heavy rains flood the ground. When the water dries up, the trees continue to grow.

A cypress swamp

A swamp in winter

16

Wet forests

A swamp offers a unique **habitat** for plants and animals because it is a combination of a wetland and a forest. The tall trees offer shelter, and the pools provide fresh water for the plants and animals. A wide variety of birds are found in swamps. The birds nest among tree branches and find food in the water below. Large animals such as moose, beavers, and alligators find homes in various swamps throughout North America.

This white-tailed deer stag looks tiny next to the heavy knees of the trees behind it.

Getting swamped

Beaver dams sometimes create new swamps by blocking the flow of water in a stream. The water has nowhere to go but out over the banks of the creek. It floods the land, creating a large pool on the surface of the ground. Few trees in the flooded area can survive when their roots are submerged because they cannot get enough air. Trees such as poplars and willows, however, easily survive in flooded conditions. Soon, they are the only trees left in the new swamp.

This beaver swims with a willow branch, which it will use to build its lodge.

Fens

Fens are shallow wetlands that are not always covered with water. They have waterlogged soil with little water showing on top. The surfaces of fens are usually flat or slightly depressed, with dips that trap water. They collect water mainly from runoff and groundwater springs.

Shallow wetlands

Fens have less water than marshes or swamps, and most of it stays below the soil's surface. During dry seasons, so much water evaporates from the fen's soil that there is room for air. As a result, hydrophytes as well as other types of plants are able to grow there. Grasses and sedges often cover fens, making them good places for animals such as deer, which **graze**, or feed, on grass. The plants also attract many small rodents, which are a source of food for owls and other birds of prey.

(right) In the middle of this fen, a bog has formed. Fens and bogs often develop near one another.

18

19

 # Bogs

Bogs get water only from precipitation. They form in areas with a lot of rain or snow and cool temperatures that slow down evaporation. Most bogs do not have water sitting on their surfaces, but the water beneath is often very deep. Bogs are so **acidic** that not many types of plants and animals survive in them. Very few decomposers can live in the acidic conditions. Without them, dead plants and animals break down slowly and layers of dead matter pile up. As the layers pile up, those on the bottom become tightly squeezed and form a material called **peat**. This material stores large amounts of water and oxygen, so some people buy peat and spread it in their gardens to help their plants grow. Since peat takes a long time to develop, bogs and other areas with peat deposits are destroyed because people **harvest**, or take, it faster than it forms.

Hungry plants

Bogs are home to some unusual plants. Bladderworts, pitcher plants, sundews, and other **carnivorous plants** need more nutrients than the bog's soil provides. They have special features that allow them to trap and eat insects! Once an insect is caught, the plants release digestive juices, which turn the insect's soft parts into a liquid that the plants then absorb.

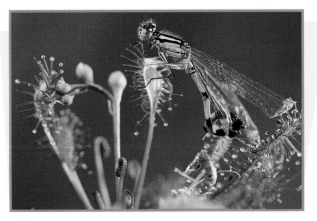
Sundews trap prey on their sticky flowers.

Clean and dry

Sphagnum moss is a plant found in bogs and some fens. This moss can absorb a great deal of liquid, and people use it in many ways. Recently, it has been used to clean up oil spills! Sphagnum moss also fights bacteria, which makes it ideal for covering cuts, scrapes, and other wounds.

Types of bogs

A **quaking bog** has a surface that looks like solid ground, but it actually covers a pool of water. A **raised bog** forms when the lower layers of peat become so tightly packed that they stop water from draining through them, and a pool forms. A new layer of peat then forms a dome over the pool of water. In cool climates, a **blanket bog** forms on a flat surface or slight slope.

This pitcher plant is surrounded by sphagnum moss. Pitcher plants have slippery, sloping leaves. Insects slide down the leaves and drown in liquid at the bottom.

Salt marshes

Saline wetlands are slightly different from freshwater marshes, swamps, and fens. Most are found along the coasts of oceans and seas, and their water is usually salty or a mix of salt and fresh water.

It's that time again!

Salt marshes are saline wetlands. Most are **coastal**, or found along coastlines. Unlike freshwater wetlands, coastal salt marshes are covered by water only half the time. The **tides** of the ocean rise and fall every day. During high tide, much of a coastal wetland is underwater. At low tide, the water moves out and the soil is no longer underwater.

Salt water from the ocean seeps underground and feeds this salt marsh.

Getting salty

Inland saline wetlands form away from oceans and seas, most often in very hot climates. All water contains small amounts of salt and other minerals. When water in an inland marsh evaporates, it leaves behind what little salt it contained. When the water evaporates faster than it is replaced in the wetland, the water that remains contains more salt than usual.

The flamingo is often found in the salty waters of inland saline wetlands.

A coastal wetland forms

Most salt marshes develop on sheltered **tidal flats**, which are the gently sloping areas along coasts that are revealed when the tide goes out. Many freshwater streams and rivers drain into the ocean. They usually carry a lot of rich sediment, which the ocean's tides then leave on the tidal flats.

The sediment gives tidal flats the nutrients and minerals that plants need. Before long, sea grasses start to grow. Their roots trap more sediment, and the soil slowly gets thicker and richer. Over time, many types of plants begin to grow. Animals including crustaceans and wading birds soon make the salt marsh their home.

Saline wetlands are very important to coastlines. They act as a buffer between the land and the ocean by breaking waves before they hit the shore and by filtering runoff water before it flows into the ocean.

Mangrove swamps

The mudskipper is an unusual fish that can climb the arched roots of mangrove trees and stay out of the water for short periods of time.

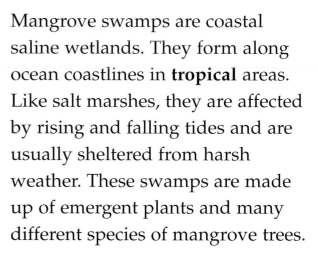

Mangrove swamps are coastal saline wetlands. They form along ocean coastlines in **tropical** areas. Like salt marshes, they are affected by rising and falling tides and are usually sheltered from harsh weather. These swamps are made up of emergent plants and many different species of mangrove trees.

Plants and animals die if too much salt builds up in them. The living things in saline wetlands must release extra salt. Mangrove trees store the salt from saline water in their leaves. The leaves then drop off, and the salt is released.

Hippopotamuses live in the mangrove swamps of Africa.

Life in a mangrove swamp

The first plants to grow in a mangrove swamp are sea grasses, which trap sediment. When enough rich soil builds up, the seeds of mangrove trees can take root. As the trees get bigger, their roots form tangled arches above the water. The roots provide shelter for a variety of animals and also trap more sediment. Soon, even more kinds of mangrove trees begin to grow. They reach different heights, and their roots grow in different shapes above and below the water. The habitat that results provides homes and hiding places for a variety of birds, along with mammals such as monkeys and bats.

Red and black mangrove trees are the first to grow in this newly forming swamp.

Dangers to wetlands

Until recently, most people believed that wetlands were useless areas because they were not able to farm them or build on them. They often drained wetlands to make way for new farms, roads, and buildings. Since the 1600s, people have destroyed more than half the world's wetlands. Today, people are realizing that these areas play an important role in our environment, but wetlands are not out of danger yet! It is now illegal to drain wetlands in many areas, but governments in some areas still encourage the draining of wetlands for farming. Around the world, pollution threatens the health of wetlands and their wildlife.

Water pollution

Although many wetland plants are able to absorb pollution, they cannot filter all of it from the water. As more pollution enters a wetland, the plants absorb greater amounts of it. The plants soon die, and the water is no longer filtered. The animals that rely on the wetland for their drinking water become sick from the pollution.

Up the chain

Many pollutants, such as pesticides, dissolve in water and seep into wetlands. In large amounts, these materials become poisonous to plants and animals. The amount of poison in animals' bodies increases with each link of a food chain. For instance, insects take in only a tiny amount of pollution. Fish eat a lot of insects, however, and end up with more pollution in their bodies as a result. Animals that feed on fish, such as birds and bears, eat several fish and end up with even more poison in their bodies. Sometimes the amount of poison is high enough to kill the animal. Many North American birds of prey are **endangered** as a result of this process of **biomagnification**.

*When wetlands are drained, their soil is useful for farming for only a short time. Before long, the land becomes dry and must be **irrigated**, or watered artificially.*

Many birds die from eating fish that have pollutants in their bodies. When links in a food chain disappear, every other part suffers.

Saving the "glades"

The Everglades is a huge freshwater wetland in Florida. It is made up of marsh and swamp areas that provide food and shelter for many types of wildlife, including the great blue heron and the American alligator, shown on the opposite page. Cypress, palm, oak, and mangrove trees, along with a wide variety of plant species, also survive in the swampy conditions.

Moving in

In the Everglades, summer is the rainy season and winter is the dry season. Some animals leave during the dry season, but others bury themselves in the mud until the rain begins again. To survive the dry season, alligators dig **gator holes**, which fill with water. Many animals, including fish, turtles, and snails, move in with the alligators until the rain begins again. Turtles sometimes lay their eggs in gator holes!

The wood stork is just one of the many endangered species that lives in the Everglades.

Drained away

In the 1900s, few people realized what a unique and important habitat the Everglades is. They drained large areas of the wetland to build houses on the land and then constructed dams to direct water away from the new homes. The homes of many plants and animals were destroyed. Drainage and clearing continued until governments realized that many Everglades animals cannot live anywhere else. The loss of their habitat made them endangered.

Preserving this wetland

Once the value of the Everglades was recognized, people began making an effort to preserve the wetland. Part of the Everglades is now a National Park. All animals and plants in it are protected by the government.

Protected enough?

The Everglades are protected, but they are still threatened by pollution. If damage from pollution continues, the habitat of many unique species may be destroyed.

The world needs wetlands

Wetlands provide a safe nesting place for migrating birds and they give babies such as these wood ducklings time to grow.

Wetlands are necessary for a healthy planet. They filter pollution from water and reduce flood damage by absorbing huge amounts of rainfall. They prevent **erosion**, or the loss of soil and shorelines. Wetlands also provide animals with places to live and breed. More than one third of threatened and endangered species make their homes in wetlands!

Keeping cool

The peat in bogs may help reduce global warming by lowering the amount of carbon dioxide in the atmosphere. Carbon dioxide is a **greenhouse gas**—it traps the sun's heat against the Earth and makes temperatures rise. In the last hundred years, people have caused the amount of carbon dioxide in the atmosphere to increase by burning **fossil fuels** such as coal and gasoline. Many scientists believe that peat absorbs much of the excess carbon dioxide and helps slow down global warming.

Keeping track

The white marker in this marsh measures the water level. During heavy rainfalls, wetlands absorb water and release it slowly. When wetlands are destroyed, however, the water is not absorbed and floods may damage surrounding communities.

Working for wetlands

As people recognize the value of wetlands, they start to create programs to protect them. Many groups work to restore wetlands that have been drained. When a wetland environment is restored, the animals that once lived there return quickly. If it is protected, a wetland habitat can thrive for many years.

See for yourself

Wetlands are used by many migrating birds as rest stations. Birds also stay in wetlands to breed and raise their young. Visit a wetland near your home and look for different species of birds. Remember never to touch or disturb any animals you find and do not leave behind any garbage!

Learn more

If you want to help protect wetlands, learn as much as you can about them. Find out what choices you and your family can make in order to reduce water pollution. Learn about local programs to protect or restore wetlands. Visit these websites to learn more:

www.ag.iastate.edu/centers/iawetlands/Kidshome.html

www.wetland.org/kids/Kids.htm

www.fws.gov/kids

Glossary

Note: Boldfaced words that are defined in the book may not appear in the glossary.

acidic Describing soil with high levels of natural acids, which prevent the growth of many plants

amphibian A cold-blooded animal that lives in water and on land

breed To create offspring

camouflage Colors or markings on an animal's body that help it blend in with its surroundings

carbon dioxide A gas that is used by plants for photosynthesis

carnivorous plant A plant that eats insects

condense To concentrate water droplets from gas into liquid form

crustacean An arthropod with a hard shell and jointed legs

endangered Describing a species that may soon disappear from Earth

evaporate To disperse water droplets from liquid to gas form

food chain A pattern of eating and being eaten

fossil fuel A natural gas

habitat A natural place in which a plant or animal is found

mammal A warm-blooded animal that gives birth to live young

microscopic Describing an organism so small that it can only be seen with a microscope

nutrient A substance that living things get from food that is needed for growth and good health

oxygen A gas in air that animals need to survive

pesticide A chemical that kills insects

pollinate To spread pollen from one plant to another, allowing seeds to be made

pollution A substance that dirties or destroys the environment

predator An animal that hunts and kills other animals for food

reptile A cold-blooded animal that lays eggs

tide The flow of water in the sea, caused by the pull of gravity from the sun and moon

tropical Describing a region near the equator

water cycle The cycle of water in gas, liquid, and solid forms

Index

3 4 5 6 7 8 9 0   Printed in the U.S.A.   2 1 0 9 8 7 6